CANTONESE
Made Nice & Easy!™

**Staff of Research & Education Association
Carl Fuchs, Language Program Director**

**Based on Language Courses developed by the
U.S. Government for Foreign Service Personnel**

 *Research & Education Association*
61 Ethel Road West
Piscataway, New Jersey 08854

Dr. M. Fogiel, Director

CANTONESE MADE NICE & EASY™

Copyright © 2001 by Research & Education Association. This copyright does not apply to the information included from U.S. Government publications, which was edited by Research & Education Association.

Printed in the United States of America

Library of Congress Control Number 2001088163

International Standard Book Number 0-87891-403-X

LANGUAGES MADE NICE & EASY is a trademark of Research & Education Association, Piscataway, New Jersey 08854

What This Guide Will Do For You

Whether travelling to a foreign country or to your favorite international restaurant, this *Nice & Easy* guide gives you just enough of the language to get around and be understood. Much of the material in this book was developed for government personnel who are often assigned to a foreign country on a moment's notice and need a quick introduction to the language.

In this handy and compact guide, you will find useful words and phrases, popular expressions, common greetings, and the words for numbers, money, and time. Every word or phrase is accompanied with the correct pronunciation and Chinese characters or writing. There is a vocabulary list for finding words quickly.

Generous margins on the pages allow you to make notes and remarks that you may find helpful.

If you expect to travel to Hong Kong, the section on the country's history and relevant up-to-date facts will make your trip more informative and enjoyable. By keeping this guide with you, you'll be well prepared to understand as well as converse in Cantonese.

Carl Fuchs
Language Program Director

Contents

Hong Kong Facts and History v

Special Points 3

How to Use the Phrase Book 4

Fill-In Sentences 6

Emergency Expressions 7

General Expressions 13

Phrases to Help Understanding 15

Personal Needs 24

Location and Terrain 48

Roads and Transportation 57

Communications 66

Numbers, Size, Time, Etc. 77

Weights and Measures 86

Important Signs 88

Alphabetical Word List 90

HONG KONG

FACTS & HISTORY

Official Name: Hong Kong Special Administrative Region

Geography
Area: 1,092 sq. km.; Hong Kong Island, Kowloon, the New Territories, and numerous small islands comprise Hong Kong.
Terrain: Hilly to mountainous, with steep slopes and natural harbor.
Climate: Tropical monsoon. Cool and humid in winter, hot and rainy from spring through summer, warm and sunny in fall.

People
Population: 6.782 million.
Population growth rate: 2.5%.
Ethnic groups: Chinese—95%, other—5%.
Religions: Approximately 43% participate in some form of religious practice. Christian—about 8%.
Languages: Cantonese (a dialect of Chinese) and English

are official. *Literacy*—92% (96% male, 88% female).
Health: *Infant mortality rate*—3.1/1,000. *Life expectancy*—79.8 yrs. (77.2 yrs. males, 82.4 yrs. females). *Work force*: 3.5 million. Wholesale, retail, and import/export trades and restaurants and hotels—45%; manufacturing—11%; finance, insurance, real estate, and business services—18%.

Government
Type: Special Administrative Region (SAR) of China, with its own mini-constitution (The Basic Law).
Branches: *Executive*—Executive Council, serving in an advisory role for the Chief Executive. *Legislative*—Legislative Council elected in September 2000. *Judicial*—Court of Final Appeal.
Subdivisions: Hong Kong, Kowloon, New Territories.

Economy
GDP (1999): $158 billion.
GDP real growth rate (1999): 3.1%.
Per capita income (1999): $23,068.
Natural resources: Outstanding deepwater harbor, feldspar.
Agriculture: *Products*—vegetables, poultry.
Industry: *Types*—textiles, clothing, tourism, electronics, plastics, toys, watches, clocks.
Trade: *Exports*—$173 billion: clothing, electronics,

textiles, watches and clocks, office machinery. *Main partners*—China, U.S., Japan, Germany, United Kingdom, Taiwan. *Imports*—$178.6 billion: consumer goods, raw materials and semi-manufactures, capital goods, foodstuffs, fuels. *Main partners*—China, Japan, Taiwan, U.S., Singapore, South Korea.

People & Language

Hong Kong's population has increased steadily over the past decade, reaching about 6.8 million by 1999. Hong Kong is one of the most densely populated areas in the world, with an overall density of some 6,300 people per square kilometer.

Cantonese, the official Chinese dialect, is spoken by most of the population. English, also an official language, is widely understood; it is spoken by more than one-third of the population. Every major religion is practiced in Hong Kong; ancestor worship is predominant due to the strong Confucian influence.

All children are required by law to be in full-time education between the ages of 6 and 15. Preschool education for most children begins at age 3. Primary school begins normally at the age of 6 and lasts for 6 years. At about age 12, children progress to a 3-year course of junior secondary education. Most stay on for a 2-year senior secondary course, while others join full-time vocational training. More than 90% of children complete upper secondary education or equivalent vocational education.

History of Hong Kong

According to archaeological studies initiated in the 1920s, human activity on Hong Kong dates back over five millennia. Excavated Neolithic artifacts suggest an influence from northern Chinese Stone-Age cultures, including the Longshan. The territory was settled by Han Chinese during the seventh century, A.D., evidenced by the discovery of an ancient tomb at Lei Cheung Uk in Kowloon. The first major migration from northern China to Hong Kong occurred during the Ching Dynasty (960-1279).

The British East India Company made the first successful sea venture to China in 1699, and Hong Kong's trade with British merchants developed rapidly soon after. After the Chinese defeat in the First Opium War (1839-1842), Hong Kong was ceded to Britain in 1842 under the Treaty of Nanking. Britain was granted a perpetual lease on the Kowloon Peninsula under the

1860 Convention of Beijing, which formally ended hostilities in the Second Opium War (1856-1858).

The United Kingdom, concerned that Hong Kong could not be defended unless surrounding areas were also under British control, executed a 99-year lease of the New Territories in 1898, significantly expanding the size of the Hong Kong colony.

In the late 19th and early 20th centuries, Hong Kong developed as a warehousing and distribution center for U.K. trade with southern China. After the end of World War II and the communist takeover of Mainland China in 1949, hundreds of thousands of people emigrated from China to Hong Kong. This helped Hong Kong become an economic success and a manufacturing, commercial, and tourism center. High life expectancy, literacy, per capita income, and other socioeconomic measures attest to Hong Kong's achievements over the last four decades.

Government

According to The Basic Law, Hong Kong's "Mini-constitution," the Legislative Council has 30 directly elected members—24 members elected by functional (occupational) constituencies and 6 elected by an Election Committee. The 1998 and 2000 elections were seen as free, open, and widely contested. There was discontent among mainly prodemocracy politicians that the functional constituency and Election Committee elections are essentially undemocratic because so few voters are eligible to vote. The Civil Service maintains its quality and neutrality, operating without discernible direction from Beijing.

Political Conditions

On July 1, 1997, China resumed the exercise of sovereignty over Hong Kong, ending more than 150 years of British colonial control. Hong Kong is a Special Administrative Region of the People's Republic of China with a high degree of autonomy in all matters except foreign and defense affairs. According to the Sino-British Joint Declaration (1984) and The Basic Law—Hong Kong's mini-constitution—for 50 years after reversion Hong Kong will retain its political, economic, and judicial systems and unique way of life and continue to participate in international agreements and organizations under the name, "Hong Kong, China."

Although concerns about the continued independence of the judiciary arose when the Hong Kong

Government sought interpretation of The Basic Law from the National People's Congress following a controversial Court of Final Appeal ruling (the Right of Abode case), Hong Kong's courts remain independent and the rule of law is respected. Hong Kong remains a free and open society where human rights are generally respected.

Economy

After a slump caused by the regionwide Asian financial crisis that began in 1997, Hong Kong's economy is on the rebound. Real gross domestic product (GDP) growth was 3.1% in 1999 and reached double digits in 2000. After peaking at 6.3% in 1999, the unemployment rate eased back to 4.8% in 2000.

In August 1998, the government intervened in the stock, futures, and currency markets to fend off "manipulators," terming the move a one-time divergence from its usual adherence to noninterventionist, market-oriented policies. The banking sector remains solid, and the government is committed to the U.S.-Hong Kong dollar link.

Hong Kong has little arable land and virtually no natural resources, including water for agriculture.

Agriculturally, it is less than 20% self-sufficient. However, its magnificent harbor has facilitated rapid development of foreign trade. Hong Kong's principal trading partners include China, the United States, Japan, Taiwan, Germany, Singapore, and South Korea. Hong Kong enjoyed economic growth in the past because of its strong manufacturing sector, but in recent years the service sector has surpassed it in importance and now accounts for 85% of GDP. The major components of Hong Kong's service trade are shipping, civil aviation, tourism, and various financial services.

Hong Kong has one of the world's most sophisticated telecommunications and information technology infrastructures and functions as a major regional and international financial and commercial center. In 1999, Hong Kong's GDP was $158 billion.

Foreign Relations

Hong Kong's foreign relations and defense are the responsibility of China. China has granted Hong Kong considerable autonomy in economic and commercial relations. Hong Kong continues to be an active, independent member of the World Trade Organization (WTO) and the Asia-Pacific Economic Cooperation (APEC) forum.

U.S. - Hong Kong Relations

U.S. policy toward Hong Kong, grounded in a determination to help preserve Hong Kong's prosperity, autonomy, and way of life, is stated in the Hong Kong Policy Act of 1992. The United States encourages high-level visits to Hong Kong as evidence of close ties and the importance of Hong Kong to U.S. interests.

The United States has substantial economic and social ties with Hong Kong. There are some 1,100 U.S. firms, including more than 400 regional operations, and 50,000 American residents in Hong Kong. According to U.S. Government statistics, U.S. exports to Hong Kong totaled U.S. $12.6 billion in 1999 and two-way trade totaled U.S. $23.1 billion, making Hong Kong the United States' 15th-largest trading partner. U.S. direct investment in Hong Kong at the end of 1999 totaled approximately U.S. $20.8 billion, making the United States one of Hong Kong's largest investors, along with the U.K., China, and Japan.

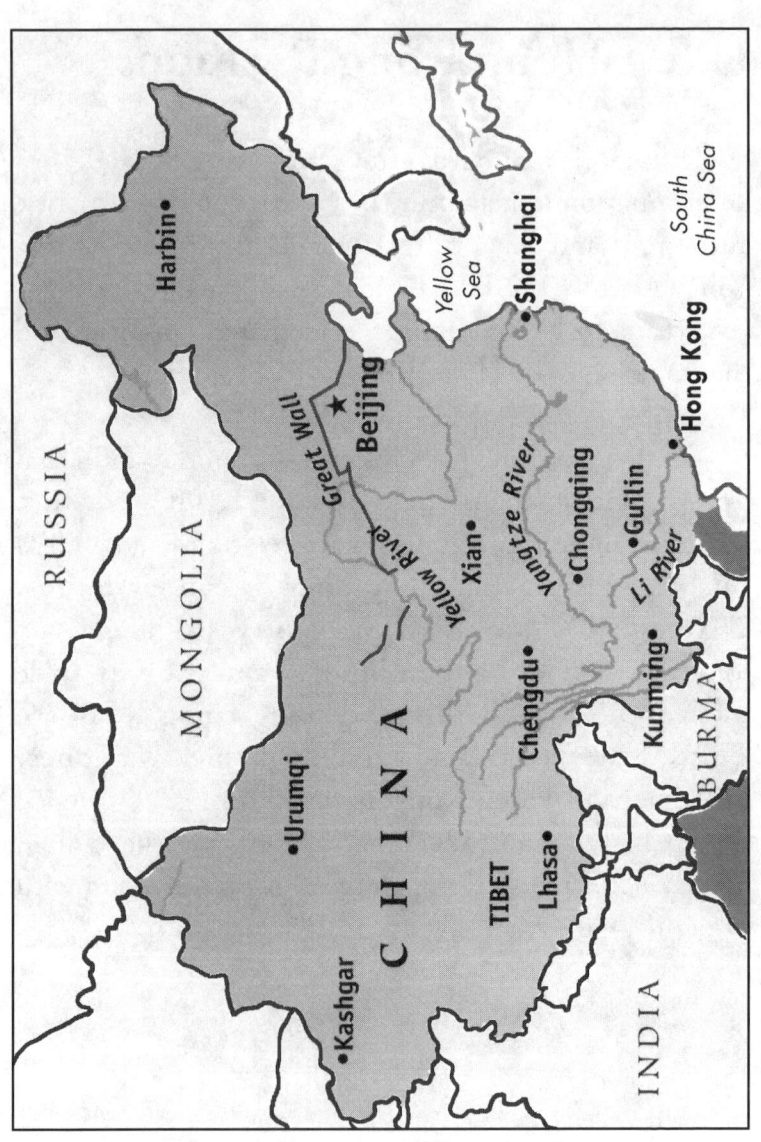

Entranceway Into Po Lin Monastery, On Lantau Island

Deities In Three Buddha Temple In Central Hong Kong

"Turtledove on Flowering Branch," Chiang T'ing-hsi

This Phrase Book contains the Cantonese words and expressions you are most likely to need. *All the words are written in a spelling which you read like English.* Each letter or combination of letters is used for the sound it normally represents in English and it *always* stands for the same sound. Thus, "oo" is always to be read as in *too*, *boot*, *tooth*, *roost*, never as in *blood* or in *door*.

Curved lines (‿) are used to show sounds that are pronounced together without any break; for example, "GA‿OO" meaning "help."

Special Points

EH   like *e* in *let*, *met*, *men*. Example: "jeh" meaning "thanks."

U   like *u* in *sun*, *dull*. Example: "YUM" meaning "drink."

<u>OO</u>	when underlined stands for a sound a little different from the *oo* of *too* and *boot*. To make it round your lips as though to say *oo* and without moving them say *ee* instead. Example: *yoo͜_OO* meaning "fish."
ER	something like the *er* sound in *her*. Example: "HER" meaning "go."

Speaking Cantonese is a little like singing. Sometimes people will not understand you if you give the wrong tune to an expression. In this Phrase Book the tones used in speaking Cantonese are written as follows:

Tone	*Example*	*Meaning*
High (capital italics)	*SEEN-SAHNG*	Sir
Middle (plain capitals)	HER	Go
Low (small italics)	*yee*	Two
Very low (small letters)	sang	City

How to Use the Phrase Book

The Table of Contents lists the situations covered. Try to become familiar with the contents of the Phrase Book so that you know where to find a given section when you need it. In each section you will find a number of questions, each one so phrased that the Cantonese speaker can give a simple answer, point out the direction, give you a number, etc. The Cantonese do not reply simply "Yes" or "No," but make a short statement answering the question. The answers you are most likely to get are given after each question or group of questions. If you don't get an answer you can understand, use one of the following expressions:

English	Pronunciation
Show me	BAY‿EE ngaw‿aw TAH‿EE-ha‿ah
Write it	seh‿eh-CHERT-loy
Write the number	seh‿eh-CHERT ho-SO loy

You can also point to the question in Cantonese and ask the Cantonese speaker to point to the answer:

Point to the answer in this book	ha‿EE NEE bo SOO‿OO WUN-CHERT dahp-AWN loy

You will find that you get along best with the Cantonese if you remember to say "please" whenever you ask them to do anything. Therefore, memorize the expression for "please," which is:

English	Pronunciation
Please	CHING nay‿ee
Please write it	CHING nay‿ee seh‿eh-CHERT-loy

It is a good idea to memorize the numbers (at least up to ten) and the other expressions you will constantly need.

When you need only a single word or expression, use the Alphabetical Word List at the back of the book.

Fill-in Sentences

Many of the expressions are given in the form of fill-in sentences, each containing a blank which you fill in with any of the words in the list that follows. For example, if you want to know where the station is, you can look either in the section headed Location or in the one headed Roads and Transportation. You will find an expression for "Where is ___?" and, in the list following it, the word for "station." Then combine the two as follows:

Where is ___?	___ ha‿EE BEEN-do AH
the station	FAW‿AW-CHEH‿EH-jahm
Where is the station?	FAW‿AW-CHEH‿EH-jahm ha‿EE BEEN-do AH

Sometimes the blank has to be filled out by the name of a city or of a person. For example:

How far is ___?	___ ya‿oo GAY‿EE y<u>oo</u>N AH
___ wants to see you	___ YEE‿OO GEEN nay‿ee

Performance At The Miramar Restaurant And Theater

EMERGENCY EXPRESSIONS

ASKING HELP

English	Pronunciation	Chinese Writing
Help!	GA‿OO *mang* AH	救命呀
Help me	CHI*NG* nay‿ee *BA*W*NG* ngaw‿aw	請你幫我
I am lost	ngaw‿aw mm *SIK lo*	我唔識路
Do you understand?	ming mm ming-*bahk* AH	明唔明白呀
I understand	ming-*bahk*	明白
I don't understand	mm ming-*bahk*	唔明白
Speak slowly	CHI*NG* nay‿ee GAW*NG* *mahn-DEE*	請你講慢的
Say it again	CHI*NG* nay‿ee *joy* GAW*NG*-GWAW	請你再講過

English	Pronunciation	Chinese Writing
Please	CHI*NG* nay⌣ee	請你
Where is a town?	sang ha⌣EE *BEEN-do* AH	城喺邊度呀
Please show me the way	CHI*NG* nay⌣ee DAH⌣EE ngaw⌣aw HER	請你帶我去
Draw me a map	CHI*NG* nay⌣ee *wahk* JE*R*NG *day*-to BAY⌣EE ngaw⌣aw	請你畫張地圖俾我
I am an American	ngaw⌣aw ha⌣ee may⌣ee-GWAWK yun	我係美國人
There are	ya⌣oo	有
There aren't	mo⌣oh	冇
Where are they?	ker-*day* ha⌣EE *BEEN-do* AH	佢哋係邊度呀
How can I get there?	DEEM *yer*NG HER AH	點樣去呀
Is there a train?	ya⌣oo mo⌣oh FAW⌣*AW-*CHEH⌣EH HER AH	有冇火車去呀
Is there a bus?	ya⌣oo mo⌣oh GOO*NG*-goong HAY-CHEH⌣EH AH	有冇公共汽車呀

English	Pronunciation	Chinese Writing
There is	ya‿oo	有
There isn't	mo‿oh	冇
Where is the station?	FAW‿AW-CHEH‿EH-jahm ha‿EE BEEN-do AH	火車站喺邊度呀
Where can I get the bus?	GOONG-goong HAY-CHEH‿EH ha‿EE BEEN-do DAHP AH	公共汽車喺邊度搭呀

A Courtyard Within Po Lin Monastery On Lantau

English	Pronunciation	Chinese Writing
Take me there	CHI*NG* nay‿*ee* DAH‿EE ngaw‿*aw* HER	請你帶我去
I want to eat	ngaw‿*aw* YEE‿OO *sik* yeh‿*eh*	我要食野
I want water	ngaw‿*aw* YEE‿OO SE*R*	我要水
Where can I get food?	*B*EEN-*do* ya‿*oo* yeh‿*eh sik* AH	邊度有野食呀
Take me to a doctor	CHI*NG* nay‿*ee* DAH‿EE ngaw‿*aw* HER YEE-SUNG-*do*	請你帶我去醫生度
Bring a doctor	CHI*NG* nay‿ee WU*N* GAW YEE-SUNG loy	請你搵個醫生來
Bring help!	WU*N* yun loy *B*AWNG-SA‿*OO*	搵人來幫手

Dragon Boat Races in Hong Kong Harbor

A 110-foot Statue Of Buddha In Po Lin Monastery

Pagoda In The Tiger Balm Gardens - Soong Dynasty

GENERAL EXPRESSIONS

GREETINGS

English	Pronunciation	Chinese Writing
Hello *or* How are you?	nay ee HO OH MA	你好嗎
I am well	ngaw aw HO OH HO OH	我好好
Thank you	DAW AW jeh	多謝
You are welcome	mm-HO OH hahk HAY	唔好客氣
Please	CHI*NG* nay ee	請你
Pardon me	DER mm j*oo*	對唔住
Sir *or* Mr.	SEEN-SAH*NG*	先生
Madam *or* Mrs.	AH-SU*M*	亞嬸
Miss	SEE OO-JEH EH	小姐
My name is ___	ngaw aw ha ee ___	我係――
What is your name?	GWA EE SING ming AH	貴姓名呀

13

English	Pronunciation	Chinese Writing
Glad to meet you	GA‿OO yerng	久仰
Come in	yup loy	入來
Sit down	CHING chaw‿aw	請坐
here	NEE-do	呢度
there	GAW‿AW-do	個度
Make yourself comfortable	mm-HO‿OH hahk HAY	唔好客氣
Are you ___?	nay‿ee ___	你——
hungry	to‿oh ngaw MA	肚餓嗎
thirsty	GANG HAWT MA	頸渴嗎
Good-by	joy GEEN	再見
See you later	DUNG juN GEEN	等陣見
See you tomorrow	TING-yut GEEN	聽日見

Restaurant Facade In Aberdeen

PHRASES TO HELP UNDERSTANDING

Yes *and* No

There are no words for Yes and No in Cantonese. Questions which would be answered by Yes and No in English are asked in an altogether different way by the Cantonese. Instead of saying "Are you a friend?" they say "You be, not be friend." The answer is either "Be" or "Not be." Here are some examples of how this works:

Question:
    Are you a friend? (You be, not be friend)   nay‿ee   ha‿ee
                                                                            mm   ha‿ee pung-ya‿oo

Positive Answer: Be   ha‿ee

Negative Answer: Not be   mm   ha‿ee

Question:
    Do you know? (You know, not know)   nay‿ee   SIK
                                                           mm   SIK

Positive Answer: Know   SIK

Negative Answer: Not know   mm   SIK

Question:
    Is there any food? (Have, lack food)   ya‿oo   mo‿oh sik-mut

Positive Answer:	Have	ya‿oo
Negative Answer:	Lack	mo‿oh

Notice that the word for "not" is "mm." The word "mo‿oh," meaning "lack" or "not have," is used when you want to say "There isn't any" or "There aren't any."

English	*Pronunciation*	*Chinese Writing*
Maybe	waȟk-JEH‿EH	或者
Certainly	*Y UT*-ding	一定
I don't know	ngaw‿aw mm *SIK*	我唔識
I think so	dah‿ee-GOY ha‿ee	大概係
I don't think so	dah‿ee-GOY mm ha‿ee	大概唔係
What languages do you speak?	nay‿ee woo‿ee GAW*NG MUT*-yeh‿eh wa‿AH AH	你會講乜野話呀
Do you speak ___?	nay‿ee woo‿ee mm woo‿ee GAW*NG* ___ AH	你會唔會講——呀
Cantonese	GWAW*NG-DOO*NG wa‿AH	廣東話
Mandarin	GWAWK-y*oo*‿*oo*	國語

English	Pronunciation	Chinese Writing
I do	woo⌣ee	會
I don't	mm woo⌣ee	唔會
I speak ——	ngaw⌣aw woo⌣ee GAWNG ——	我會講——
I don't speak well	ngaw⌣aw GAWNG-DUK mm HO⌣OH	我講得唔好
Can you get an interpreter?	nay⌣ee nung-GA⌣OO WUN GAW choon-wa⌣AH loy MA	你能夠搵個傳話來嗎
I can	nung-GA⌣OO	能夠
I can't	mm nung-GA⌣OO	唔能夠
I don't understand	ngaw⌣aw mm ming-bahk	我唔明白
Speak slowly	CHING nay⌣ee GAWNG mahn-DEE	請你講慢的
Do you understand?	nay⌣ee ming mm ming-bahk AH	你明唔明白呀
I understand	ming-bahk	明白
I don't understand	mm ming-bahk	唔明白
What?	MUT-yeh⌣eh	乜野

English	Pronunciation	Chinese Writing
Repeat	CHI*NG* nay‿ee joy GAW*NG*-GWAW	請你再講過
What do you call this?	*NEE-DEE* GEE‿OO *MUT*-yeh‿eh	呢的叫乜野
What is this?	*NEE-DEE* ha‿ee *MUT*-yeh‿eh	呢的係乜野
What is that?	GAW‿*AW-DEE* ha‿ee *MUT*-yeh‿eh	個的係乜野
Wait a moment	*DUNG YUT* ju*N*	等一陣
Come with me	*GUN* ngaw‿aw loy	跟我來
___ wants to see you	___ YEE‿OO GEEN nay‿ee	——要見你
I want to ask you questions	ngaw‿aw YEE‿OO mun-mun nay‿ee	我要問問你
Show me	CHI*NG* nay‿ee BAY‿*EE* ngaw‿aw TAH‿*EE*-ha‿ah	請你俾我睇吓
Write it	seh‿eh-CHERT-loy	寫出來
Write the number	seh‿eh-CHERT ho-SO loy	寫出號數來

English	Pronunciation	Chinese Writing
Write the numbers English style	CHI*NG* nay‿ee yoong AH-LAH‿EE-BAHK jee-mo‿oh seh‿eh-CHERT ho-SO loy	請你用亞拉伯字母寫出號數來

NOTE: For Chinese numbers see pages 69-70.

English	Pronunciation	Chinese Writing
Point to the answer in this book	ha‿EE NEE bo SOO‿OO WUN-CHERT dahp-AWN loy	喺呢部書搵出答案來
Draw a picture of it	CHI*NG* nay‿ee wahk-CHERT-loy	請你畫出來

QUESTIONS ABOUT AN INDIVIDUAL

English	Pronunciation	Chinese Writing
Are you ___?	nay‿ee ha‿ee mm ha‿ee ___ AH	你係唔係――呀
Chinese	JOONG-GWAWK yun	中國人
Cantonese	GWAWNG-DOONG yun	廣東人
I am	ha‿ee	係
I'm not	mm ha‿ee	唔係

English	Pronunciation	Chinese Writing
Where are you from?	nay ee ha ee BEEN-do yun AH	你係邊度人呀
I am from ___	ngaw aw ha ee ___ yun	我係――人
Where do you live?	nay ee joo BEEN-do AH	你住邊度呀
I live in ___	ngaw aw joo ha EE ___	我住喺――
Where are you going?	nay ee HER BEEN-do AH	你去邊度呀
I am going to ___	ngaw aw HER ___	我去――
Where are your friends?	nay ee-GEH pung-ya oo ha EE BEEN-do AH	你嘅朋友喺邊度呀
Are they ___?	ker-day ha EE mm ha EE ___ AH	佢地喺唔喺――呀
near	JAW AW-GUN	左近
far	HO OH yoon	好遠
Where is your ___?	nay ee-GEH ___ ha EE BEEN-do AH	你嘅――喺邊度呀

English	Pronunciation	Chinese Writing
family	*OOK*-kay‿*ee*	屋企
father	lo‿*oh*-da‿*oo*	老竇
mother	lo‿*oh*-mo‿*OH*	老母
husband	lo‿*oh*-*GOONG*	老公
wife	lo‿*oh*-paw	老婆

Hong Kong's Wanchai District

Traditional Junk With Red Sails In Hong Kong Harbor

Deities In Three Buddha Temple In Central Hong Kong

PERSONAL NEEDS

FOOD AND DRINK

English	Pronunciation	Chinese Writing
I am hungry	ngaw‿aw to‿oh ngaw	我肚餓
I am thirsty	ngaw‿aw GA*NG* HAWT	我頸渴
Where is there water?	SE*R* ha‿EE BEEN-do AH	水喺邊度呀
Where is a restaurant?	fahn-GWOO*N* ha‿EE BEEN-do AH	飯館喺邊度呀
I want to buy food	ngaw‿aw YEE‿OO mah‿ee sik-mut	我要買食物
Is this good to ___?	NEE-DEE HO‿OH mm HO‿OH ___ AH	呢的好唔好——呀
eat	sik	食
drink	YU*M*	飲
It is good	HO‿OH	好

English	Pronunciation	Chinese Writing
It isn't good	mm HO͜_OH_	唔好
I want ―	ngaw͜*aw* YEE͜OO ―	我要――
Give me ―	BAY͜*EE* ― ngaw͜*aw*	俾――我
Bring me ―	DAH͜EE ― BAY͜*EE* ngaw͜*aw*	帶――俾我
food	*sik-mut*	食物
water	SE*R*	水
beans	da͜*OO*	豆
beef	nga͜oo-*yook*	牛肉
beets	*hoong* law-*bahk*	紅蘿蔔
bread	meen-BAH͜*OO*	麵包
butter	nga͜oo-ya͜oo	牛油
cabbage	yeh-CHOY	椰菜
candy	*taw*NG	糖
cheese	CHEE-see͜*EE*	雌氏
chicken	GA͜*EE*	鷄
chocolate	J*OO*-GWOO-LERT	朱古律

25

Boats Moored At The Hong Kong Yacht Club In Aberdeen

Dragon Boat Races Held Annually In Hong Kong Harbor

English	Pronunciation	Chinese Writing
clams	hah‿ee	蟹
eggs	GA‿EE-dahN	鷄蛋
fish	*yoo‿OO*	魚
lamb	yerng-*yook*	羊肉
lentils	BEEN-da‿*oo*	扁豆
lettuce	SAHNG-CHOY	生菜
lobsters	*loong-HA*	龍蝦
meat	*yook*	肉
oysters	SAHNG-ho	生蠔
pork	J*OO*‿OO-*yook*	猪肉
potatoes	*soo*-JA‿EE	薯仔
rice (cooked)	*fahn*	飯
soup	TAWNG	湯
spinach	BAW AW-CHOY	波菜
squash	JEET-*GWA*	節瓜
steak	nga‿oo-*PA*	牛扒
tomatoes	FAHN-*keh*‿*EH*	番茄
turnips	law-*bahk*	蘿蔔
vegetables	CHOY	菜
apples	ping-GWAW‿*AW*	蘋果

English	Pronunciation	Chinese Writing
bananas	*HERNG-JEE͜OO*	香蕉
cherries	*YING*-to	櫻桃
coconuts	yeh-*JEE͜EE*	椰子
dates	*JOH͜OH*	棗
grapes	*po*-tah͜ee-*JEE͜EE*	葡提子
lemons	ning-*MOONG*	檸檬
mangoes	*MAWNG-GWAW͜AW*	芒果
oranges	*chahNG*	橙
peaches	*to͜OH*	桃
pears	*lay͜EE*	梨
pineapples	*BAW͜AW*-law	菠蘿
plums	*moo͜EE*	梅
strawberries	yerng-moo͜ee	洋梅
watermelon	*SA͜EE-GWA*	西瓜
beer	*BEH JA͜OO*	啤酒
boiled water	*GWUN SER*	滾水
brandy	but-*LAHN-day͜EE JA͜OO*	拔蘭地酒
coffee	*GA-FEH*	咖啡

English	Pronunciation	Chinese Writing
coffee with milk	GA-FEH GA‿AH nga‿oo-NAH-EE	咖啡加牛奶
cream	gay-LEEM	忌廉
drinking water	YUM-GEH SER	飲嘅水
milk	nga‿oo-NAH‿EE	牛奶
tea	cha	茶
wine	JA‿OO	酒
pepper	woo-JEE‿OO-FUN	胡椒粉
salt	yeem	鹽
sugar	tawng	糖
vinegar	CHO	醋
a cup	BOO‿EE	杯
a fork	CHA	叉
a glass	BAW-LAY BOO‿EE	玻璃杯
a knife	DO	刀
a plate	deeP	碟
a spoon	chee-GUNG	匙羹
I want it ——	ngaw‿aw YEE‿OO —— GEH	我要——嘅

English	Pronunciation	Chinese Writing
cooked	sook	熟
raw	SAHNG	生
rare	BOON SAHNG sook	半生熟
well done	sook-DEE	熟的
baked	HAWNG	烘
boiled	JOO_OO	煮
broiled or roasted	SEE_OO	燒
fried	CHAH_OO	炒

LODGING

Where is a hotel?	ler-GWOON ha EE BEEN- do AH	旅館喺邊度呀

Coxswains - Dragon Boat Races Using Drum Beat Rhythm

31

English	Pronunciation	Chinese Writing
I want to spend the night	ngaw‿aw YEE‿OO *joo* YUT mah*n*	我要住一晚
I want ___	ngaw‿aw YEE‿OO ___	我要――
a bed	chawng	床
blankets	JEEN	毡
hot water	*yeet* SE*R*	熱水
insecticide	SAHT-choong-*yerk*	殺虫藥
a light	*D*UNG-FAW‿AW	燈火
a mattress	DEEN-*yook*	墊褥
mosquito netting	M*U*N-*jer*NG	蚊帳
a pillow	JU*M*-ta‿oo	枕頭
a quilt	pay‿*ee*	被
a room	*faw*NG	房
soap	FA*H*N-GAH*N*	番梘
toilet paper	CHO‿OH-JEE‿EE	草紙
a towel	mo-G*U*N	毛巾
Where is the toilet?	CHEE-SAW‿AW ha‿EE BEEN-*do* AH	廁所喺邊度呀

English	Pronunciation	Chinese Writing
I want ___	ngaw‿aw YEE‿OO ___	我要———
to sleep	FUN-GAH‿OO	瞓覺
to wash	SA EE meen	洗面
to bathe	SA‿EE SUN	洗身
the key	SAW‿AW-see	鎖匙
Call me at ___ o'clock	CHI*NG* nay‿ee ___ DEE*M* JOO*NG* GEE‿OO ngaw‿aw	請你———點鐘叫我
Have you a message for me?	ya‿oo mo‿oh SERN-*gee*N BAY‿EE ngaw‿aw AH	有冇信件俾我呀
I have	ya‿oo	有
I haven't	mo‿oh	冇
Give this message to ___	DAH‿EE NEE FOO*NG* SERN BAY‿EE ___	帶呢封信俾———
Here's my address	NEE-GAW ha‿ee ngaw‿aw-GEH *joo*-JEE‿EE	呢個係我嘅住址
Forward mail	CHI*NG* nay‿ee JO*ON* GAY SERN	請你轉寄信

English	Pronunciation	Chinese Writing
Send my things	CHI*NG* nay‿*ee* SOONG ngaw‿*aw*-GEH yeh‿*eh* HER	請你送我嘅野去
I shall return ——	ngaw‿*aw* —— *FAH*N loy	我——返來
tomorrow	*T*I*NG*-yut	聽日
Wednesday	lah‿*ee*-BAH‿*EE* *SAH*M	禮拜三
Have you a —— room?	ya‿*oo* mo‿*oh* —— faw*NG* AH	有冇——房呀
better	HO‿*OH-DEE*-GEH	好的嘅
larger	dah‿*ee-DEE*-GEH	大的嘅
cheaper	pang-*DEE*-GEH	平的嘅
I have	ya‿*oo*	有
I haven't	mo‿*oh*	冇

MEDICAL AID

Help!	GA‿OO *mang* AH	救命呀
Where is a ——?	—— ha‿*EE* BEEN-do AH	——喺邊度呀

English	Pronunciation	Chinese Writing
Call a ___	CHI*NG* nay﹍*ee* GEE﹍OO GAW ___ loy	請你叫個——來
doctor	YEE-SUNG	醫生
dentist	nga-FAW YEE-SUNG	牙科醫生
ambulance	GA﹍OO-woo﹍*oo*-CHEH	救護車
nurse	HAWN-woo﹍*oo*	看護
first-aid man	GA﹍OO-*GUP*-GEH yun	救急嘅人
Quick!	FAH﹍EE-*DEE*	快的
Stop the bleeding	JEE﹍EE HOOT	止血
A tourniquet!	JEE﹍*EE*-HOOT-dah﹍*EE*	止血帶
Tie it here	BAW*NG* NEE-do	綁呢度
Above the wound	SER*NG*-HA﹍*OO* ser*ng*-ta﹍oo	傷口上頭
I am sick	ngaw﹍*aw* bang	我病
He is sick	ker bang	佢病
I am wounded	ngaw﹍*aw* DA﹍*AH* SER*NG*-JAW﹍*AW*	我打傷左

English	Pronunciation	Chinese Writing
He is wounded	ker DA͜_AH SERNG-JAW͜_AW	佢打傷左
My ___ hurts	ngaw͜_aw ___ TOONG	我一一痛
head	ta͜_oo	頭
tooth	nga	牙
back	BOO͜_EE-JAK	背脊
stomach	to͜_oh	肚
I am hurt here	ngaw͜_aw NEE-do SERNG-JAW͜_AW	我呢度傷左
I am hurt in the ___	ngaw͜_aw-GEH ___ SERNG-JAW͜_AW	我嘅一一傷左
He is hurt in the ___	ker-GEH ___ SERNG-JAW͜_AW	佢嘅一一傷左
head	ta͜_oo	頭
face	*meen*	面
ear	yee͜_ee-JA͜_EE	耳仔
eye	ngah*n*	眼
nose	bay-GAW	鼻哥
mouth	HA͜_OO	口

English	Pronunciation	Chinese Writing
jaw	*ha*-pa	下耙
throat	*ha*‿*oo-loong*	喉嚨
neck	GA*N*G	頸
shoulder	BAWK-ta‿oo	膊頭
arm	SA‿*OO*-BAY	手臂
elbow	SA‿*OO-JAH*NG	手踭
hand	SA‿*OO*	手
back	BOO‿EE-JAK	背脊
chest	*HOO*NG	胸
stomach	to‿*oh*	肚
hip	SEE‿*OO*-YEE*M*-GW*UT*	小掩骨
leg	TE*R*	腿
knee	*SUT*-ta‿oo	膝頭
ankle	GERK-*JAH*NG	脚踭
foot	GERK	脚
Get ___	CHI*NG* nay‿ee WU*N* ___	請你搵――
a blanket	JEEN	氈
boiled water	GWU*N* SE*R*	滾水

37

English	Pronunciation	Chinese Writing
cotton	*yerk*-meen-*FA*	藥棉花
a disinfectant	S*EE*⌣OO-*dook yerk*-SE*R*	消毒藥水
drinking water	YU*M*-GEH SE*R*	飲嘅水
hot water	*yeet* SE*R*	熱水
ice	SO͟OT	雪
a knife	*DO*	刀
a sedative	*A*WN-meen-*yerk*	安眠藥
sheets	pay⌣*ee*-DA*H*N	被單
something to bandage with	JAHT SE*R*NG-*HA*⌣*OO*-GEH BO	紮傷口嘅布
splints	*gahp-bahN*	夾板
a stimulant	*H*ING-FUN-*JAH*⌣*EE*	興奮劑
a stretcher	GA⌣OO-woo⌣*oo*-chawng	救護床
Do not touch ___	mm-HO⌣*OH DA*⌣*OO* ___	唔好抖———
Do not move ___	mm-HO⌣*OH BOO*N ___HER	唔好搬———去
Lift ___ carefully	S*EE*⌣*OO*-SUM toy-HAY ___	小心抬起———
me	ngaw⌣*aw*	我

The City's Harbor and Skyline Seen From Victoria Peak

English	Pronunciation	Chinese Writing
him	ker	佢
them	ker-day	佢地
Be careful	SEE⌣OO-SUM	小心
Do not give him that	mm-HO⌣OH BAY⌣EE GAW⌣AW-DEE ker	唔好俾個的佢

BUYING AND PERSONAL SERVICES

Where to Get It

| Where is a ___? | ___ ha⌣EE BEEN-do AH | ——喺邊度呀 |

English	Pronunciation	Chinese Writing
barber shop	TA͡EE-ta͡oo-po͡OH	剃頭鋪
bathroom	SA͡EE-SUN-fawNG	洗身房
drug store	yerk-fawng	藥房
grocery	jahp-faw-po͡OH	雜貨鋪
movie	YING-HAY-yooN	影戲院
restaurant	fahn-GWOON	飯館
tailor shop	SA͡EE-JAWNG-po͡OH	西裝鋪
I want to buy ___	ngaw͡aw YEE͡OO mah͡ee ___	我要買――
Where can I buy ___?	BEEN-do ya͡oo ___ mah͡ee	邊度有――賣

Things Wanted

Give me ___	CHING nay͡ee BAY͡EE ___ ngaw͡aw	請你俾――我
this	NEE-DEE	呢的
that	GAW͡AW-DEE	個的
one of these	YUT GAW NEE-DEE	一個呢的

English	Pronunciation	Chinese Writing
a bandage	SA‿AH-BO	紗布
a battery	*deen*-chee	電池
a belt	pay-*dah*‿EE	皮帶
a brush	ta‿oo-CHAH*T*	頭刷
buttons	na‿OO	鈕
cigarettes	YEEN-JA‿EE	烟仔
cloth	BO	布
a coat	SAHM	衫
a comb	SAW	梳
cotton	*yerk*-meen-FA	藥棉花
a disinfectant	SEE‿OO-*dook* *yerk*-SER	消毒藥水
an electric bulb	*deen*-DUNG-*dah*M	電燈胆
envelopes	SERN-*FOONG*	信封
a flashlight	*deen*-SA‿OO-DUNG	電手燈
gloves	SA‿OO-TO	手套
goggles	JEH FOONG ngah*n*-GA*NG*	遮風眼鏡
handkerchiefs	SA‿OO-GUN-JA‿EE	手巾仔
a hat	*mo*‿OH	帽

English	Pronunciation	Chinese Writing
ink	muk-SER	墨水
iodine	DEEN JA͜OO	碘酒
a knife	DO	刀
a laxative	SEH-yerk	瀉藥
matches	FAW͜AW-chah͜EE	火柴
a needle	JUM	針
an overcoat	dah͜ee-LAH͜OO	大褸
pants	foo	褲
paper	JEE͜EE	紙
a pencil	yoon-BUT	鉛筆
pins	dah͜ee-ta͜oo-JUM	大頭針
quinine	GUM-GA͜EE-nahp	金雞鈉
a raincoat	yoo͜oo-YEE	雨衣
a razor	SO͜OH-pah͜OO	鬚刨
razor blades	TA͜EE-SO-DO͜OH-PEEN	剃鬚刀片
rubbing alcohol	CHAHT SUN yoong-GEH FAW͜AW-JA͜OO	擦身用嘅火酒
a scarf	GANG-GUN	頸巾

English	Pronunciation	Chinese Writing
scissors	GAH⌣OO-JEE*N*	鉸剪
shaving cream	TA⌣EE-*SO-GO*	剃鬚膏
a shirt	SERT-*SAHM*	恤衫
shoelaces	hah⌣ee-*dah*⌣*EE*	鞋帶
shoes	hah⌣ee	鞋
soap	*FA*H*N*-GAH*N*	番梘
socks	*mut*	襪
sunglasses	JEH⌣EH *yut-ta*⌣*OO*-GEH ngah*n*-GA*NG*	遮日頭嘅眼鏡
a sweater	LAH*NG*-SAHM	冷衫
talcum powder	SAW*NG*-SUN-FU*N*	爽身粉
thread	SEEN	線
a toothbrush	nga-CHAH*T*	牙刷
toothpaste	nga-*GO*	牙膏
tooth powder	nga-FU*N*	牙粉
an undershirt	DA⌣EE-*SAHM*	底衫
undershorts	DA⌣EE-*foo*	底褲
Have you something else?	ya⌣oo mo⌣oh DA⌣EE *yee-DEE* AH	有冇第二的呀

43

English	Pronunciation	Chinese Writing
I have	ya‿oo	有
I haven't	mo‿oh	冇
More	*DAW-DEE*	多的
I want this ――	ngaw‿*aw* YEE‿OO *NEE-DEE* ――	我要呢的――

Services Wanted

English	Pronunciation	Chinese Writing
Where can I get this ――?	*NEE-DEE* NI*NG* HER BEEN-*do* ――	呢的擰去邊度――
washed	SA‿EE	洗
pressed	TAWNG	熨
dry cleaned	*GA*WN-SA‿EE	乾洗
repaired	SA‿OO-JI*NG*	修整
I want to hire ――	ngaw‿*aw* YEE‿OO JO‿OH ――	我要租――
I want to borrow ――	ngaw‿*aw* YEE‿OO *jeh* ――	我要借――
this	*NEE-DEE*	呢的
that	GAW‿*AW-DEE*	個的

English	Pronunciation	Chinese Writing
I want ___	ngaw‿aw YEE‿OO ___	我要——
a haircut	TA‿EE ta‿oo	剃頭
a shave	TA‿EE SO‿OH	剃鬚
a guide	YUT GAW yun DAH‿EE lo	一個人帶路
a porter	YUT GAW yun DAHM yeh‿eh	一個人担野
a driver	YUT GAW HAY-CHEH-FOO	一個汽車夫
a taxi	DIK-see‿EE	的士
someone to help me	YUT GAW yun BAWNG ngaw‿aw	一個人幫我

Payment

How much?	GAY‿EE DAW	幾多
How much is ___?	___ GAY‿EE DAW CHEEN AH	——幾多錢
I will pay you	ngaw‿aw ja‿oo BAY‿EE CHEEN nay‿ee	我就俾錢你

English	Pronunciation	Chinese Writing
This is American money	NEE-DEE ha‿ee may‿ee-GWAWK CHEEN	呢的係美國錢
It is worth ___	jik-DUK ___	值得——
Not so much	mo‿oh GOOM DAW	冇咁多
That's too much	TAH‿EE GWA‿EE	太貴
I will pay you ___	ngaw‿aw ja‿oo BAY‿EE nay‿ee ___	我就俾你——
No more	ja‿oo GOOM DAW	就咁多
Will you sell this for ___?	___ HUNG mm HUNG mah‿ee AH	——肯唔肯賣呀
You owe me ___	nay‿ee JAHNG ngaw‿aw ___	你掙我——
Give me a receipt	CHING nay‿ee BAY‿EE ngaw‿aw YUT JERNG SA‿OO-tee‿oo	請你俾我一張收條
Here is a receipt	NEE JERNG ja‿oo ha‿ee SA‿OO-tee‿oo	呢張就係收條

English	Pronunciation	Chinese Writing
Take it to this address	SOONG NEE-DEE yeh eh HER NEE GAW day-JEE EE	送呢的野去呢個地址
You will be paid on delivery	faw DO GAH OO CHEEN	貨到交錢

A Double-Decker Tram In Aberdeen, British Heritage

LOCATION AND TERRAIN

LOCATION

English	Pronunciation	Chinese Writing
What place is this?	NEE-do ha͡EE BEEN-do	呢度係邊度
Show me on this map	CHING nay͡ee ha͡EE NEE JERNG day-to JEE͡EE-CHERT-loy	請你喺呢張地圖指出來
Have you a map?	nay͡ee ya͡oo mo͡oh day-to AH	你有冇地圖呀
Can you draw me a map?	nay͡ee wahk JERNG day-to BAY͡EE ngaw͡uw, DUK mm DUK AH	你畫張地圖俾我，得唔得呀

English	Pronunciation	Chinese Writing
Can you guide me?	nay ee DAH EE ngaw aw HER, *DUK* mm *DUK* AH	你帶我去，得唔得呀
Can you find us a guide?	nay ee toong ngaw aw-day WUN GAW yun DAH EE lo, *DUK* mm *DUK* AH	你同我地搵個人帶路，得唔得呀
Where is ___?	___ ha EE BEEN-do AH	——喺邊度
the nearest town	JER ku*n*-GEH sang	最近嘅城
the railroad station	FAW AW CHEH EH-jah*m*	火車站
a telephone	deen-wa AH	電話
the U. S. Consulate	may ee GWAWK *l*i*n*g-see-GWOO*N*	美國領事館
the power plant	deen-*DUNG*-GOOK	電燈局
the police station	GI*NG*-CHAHT-GOOK	警察局
Is there ___ near here?	NEE-do JAW AW-gun ya oo mo oh ___	呢度左近有冇——

English	Pronunciation	Chinese Writing
a river	haw	河
a well	JANG	井
a railroad	FAW‿AW-CHEH‿EH-lo	火車路
a telephone exchange	deen-wa‿AH-GOOK	電話局
a radio station	mo‿oh-SEEN-deen-toy	無線電台
a town *or* city	sang	城
What is its name?	GEE‿OO MUT-yeh‿eh mang AH	叫乜野名呀
What other towns are there?	joong ya‿oo BEEN GAY‿EE GAW sang AH	重有邊幾個城呀
Point	CHING nay‿ee yoong SA‿OO JEE‿EE YUT JEE‿EE	請你用手指一指
Thank you	DAW‿AW jeh	多謝
Show me the way	CHING nay‿ee DAH‿EE ngaw‿aw HER	請你帶我去
Which way is north?	BEEN BEEN ha‿ee BUK	邊便係北

English	Pronunciation	Chinese Writing
This way	NEE tee‿oo lo	呢條路
That way	GAW‿AW tee‿oo lo	個條路
To the ___	HERNG ___	向——
left	JAW‿AW	左
right	ya‿oo	右
north	BUK	北
northeast	DOONG-BUK	東北
east	DOONG	東
southeast	DOONG-nahm	東南
south	nahm	南
southwest	SA‿EE-nahm	西南
west	SA‿EE	西
northwest	SA‿EE-BUK	西北
Here	NEE-do	呢度
There	GAW‿AW-do	個度

DISTANCE

How far is ___?	___ ya‿oo GAY‿EE yooN AH	——有幾遠呀

Inside Kowloon's Tsim Sha Tsui Shopping Mall

Plaster Deity Displayed Near A Repulse Bay Beach

English	Pronunciation	Chinese Writing
Is it ___?	___ mm ___ AH	——唔——呀
far	yoon	遠
near	kun	近
(Chinese) mile	lay‿ee	里
(Chinese) foot	CHAK	尺
How many (Chinese) miles from here?	lay NEE-do ya‿oo GAY‿EE DAW lay‿ee AH	離呢度有幾多里呀

NOTE: A Chinese mile is about ⅓ of a mile.
A Chinese foot is about 14 inches.

NATURE OF TERRAIN

English	Pronunciation	Chinese Writing
Are you familiar with this region?	NEE daht day-FAWNG nay‿ee sook mm sook AH	呢達地方你熟唔熟呀
I am familiar	sook	熟
I'm not familiar	mm sook	唔熟
Is it ___?	___ mm ___ AH	——唔——呀
flat	ping	平
dry	GAWN	乾
wet	SUP	溼

English	Pronunciation	Chinese Writing
Is it rocky?	sak-ta‿oo DAW‿AW mm DAW‿AW AH	石頭多唔多呀
Is it muddy?	na‿ee-BAHN DAW‿AW mm DAW‿AW AH	泥辦多唔多呀
Is it passable?	hahng mm hahng-DUK GWAW AH	行唔行得過呀
It is passable	hahng-DUK	行得
It's not passable	mm hahng-DUK	唔行得
Are there ___?	ya‿oo mo‿oh ___ AH	有冇――呀
highways	GOONG-lo	公路
hills	SAHN-JA‿EE	山仔
lakes	woo	湖
mountains	SAHN	山
passes	SAHN-lo	山路
paths	SEE‿OO-lo	小路
rivers	haw	河
roads	lo	路
springs	SER-choon	水泉

English	Pronunciation	Chinese Writing
woods	*soo*-lum	樹林
There are	ya‿*oo*	有
There aren't	mo‿*oh*	冇
Is the water deep?	SE*R* S*UM* mm S*UM* AH	水深唔深呀
Are the mountains high?	SAHN GO‿OH mm GO‿OH AH	山高唔高呀
Is the current swift?	SE*R* G*UP* mm G*UP* AH	水急唔急呀
Is there a bridge?	ya‿*oo* mo‿*oh* kee‿*oo* AH	有冇橋呀

Altar In Three Buddha Temple In Central Hong Kong

ROADS AND TRANSPORTATION

ROADS AND BRIDGES

English	Pronunciation	Chinese Writing
What town does this road lead to?	*NEE* tee‿oo *lo* HER *BEEN* GAW sang AH	呢條路去邊個城呀
Is this road ___?	*NEE* tee‿oo *lo* ___ mm ___ AH	呢條路一唔一呀
Is this bridge ___?	*NEE do* kee‿oo ___ mm ___ AH	呢度橋一唔一呀
good	HO‿*OH*	好
Is this road passable?	*NEE* tee‿oo *lo* hahng mm hahng-*DUK* GWAW AH	呢條路行唔行得過呀
Will this bridge carry this load?	*NEE do* kee‿oo sing mm sing-*DUK* HAY GOO*M* CHOONG AH	呢度橋乘唔乘得起咁重呀

57

English	Pronunciation	Chinese Writing
Are there ___?	ya‿oo mo‿oh ___ AH	有冇――呀
bridges	kee‿oo	橋
guideposts	lo-pah‿ee	路牌
guides	DAH‿EE-lo-yun	帶路人
mud puddles	na‿ee-TUM	泥冰
obstructions	JAW‿AW-ngoy	阻礙
one-way stretches	DAHN-hahng-lo	單行路
potholes	TUM	冰
ruts	CHEH‿EH lerN-YUN	車輪印
There are	ya‿oo	有
There aren't	mo‿oh	冇
What is the speed limit?	KWA‿EE-DING-GEH CHOOK-do ha‿ee GAY‿EE DAW ying-lay‿ee AH	規定嘅速度係幾多英里呀
Do you know the road?	nay‿ee SIK mm SIK lo AH	你識唔識路呀
I do know	SIK	識
I don't know	mm SIK	唔識

English	Pronunciation	Chinese Writing
Please guide us	CHI*NG* nay⌣ee DAH⌣EE ngaw⌣aw-day	請你帶我地
We will pay you	ngaw⌣aw-day woo⌣ee BAY⌣EE CHEE*N* nay⌣ee	我地會俾錢你
Where can we cross the river?	BEEN-do HAW⌣AW-yee⌣ee GWAW haw AH	邊度可以過河呀
How deep is this river?	NEE tee⌣oo haw GAY⌣EE SUM AH	呢條河幾深呀
Is the bottom ___?	haw-DA⌣EE ha⌣ee mm ha⌣ee ___ AH	河底係唔係——呀
muddy	na⌣ee	泥
rocky	sak	石
sandy	SA⌣AH	沙
It is	ha⌣ee	係
It isn't	mm ha⌣ee	唔係

RAILROADS, BUSES, PLANES

Where's the ___?	___ ha⌣EE BEEN-do AH	——喺邊度呀

English	Pronunciation	Chinese Writing
air field	FAY-GAY‿EE-cherng	飛機場
bus station	GOONG-goong HAY-CHEH‿EH-jahm	公共汽車站
railroad station	FAW‿AW-CHEH‿EH-jahm	火車站
baggage room	hahng-lay‿ee-fawNG	行李房
ticket office	mah‿ee-FAY-fawng	賣飛房
I want to go to ―	ngaw‿aw YEE‿OO HER ―	我要去――
When does a ― leave?	― GAY‿EE see‿EE HOY‿EE AH	――幾時開呀
bus	GOONG-goong HAY-CHEH‿EH	公共汽車
plane	FAY-GAY‿EE	飛機
train	FAW‿AW-CHEH‿EH	火車
When does the ― arrive?	― GAY‿EE see‿EE DO AH	――幾時到呀

English	Pronunciation	Chinese Writing
Is the ___ running?	JOONG ya‿oo mo‿oh ___ HOY‿EE AH	重有冇――開呀
It is	ya‿oo	有
It isn't	mo‿oh	冇
A ticket to ___	YUT JERNG FAY HER ___	壹張飛去――
What's the fare to ___?	HER ___ GEH lo-FAH‿EE GAY‿EE DAW AH	去――嘅路費 幾多呀
When do we get to ___?	ngaw‿aw-day GAY‿EE see‿EE DO ___ AH	我地幾時到――呀
Give me a timetable	BAY‿EE JERNG see-GAHN-BEE‿OO ngaw‿aw	俾張時間表我

OTHER MEANS OF TRANSPORTATION

Where can I find ___?	BEEN-do ya‿oo ___ AH	邊度有――呀
a bicycle	DAHN-CHEH‿EH	單車
a boat	soon	船

61

English	Pronunciation	Chinese Writing
a car	HAY-*CHEH*‿EH	汽車
a donkey	*lo*-JA‿*EE*	驢仔
a horse	ma‿*ah*	馬
a mule	ler	騾
a plane	*FAY-GAY*‿EE	飛機
a wagon	SAY-lern-*CHEH*	四輪車

REPAIRS AND SUPPLIES

English	Pronunciation	Chinese Writing
Where can I find ___?	BEEN-*do* ya‿*oo* ___ AH	邊度有——呀
a battery	*deen*-chee	電池
brake fluid	SAHT-*CHEH* EH-*ya*‿*OO*	刹車油
a cable	TEET-lahm	鐵纜
chains	TEET-*leeN*	鐵鏈
Diesel oil	ya‿oo-*JA*‿AH ya‿*OO*	油揸油
distilled water	JING-*lah*‿*oo* SE*R*	蒸溜水
an electric bulb	*deen*-D*UNG*-dah*M*	電燈膽
an electrician	*deen*-HAY *GOO*NG-yun	電器工人

English	Pronunciation	Chinese Writing
a filling station	*TEEM-ya͜OO-*jah*m*	添油站
a garage	*CHEH͜EH-*faw*NG*	車房
gasoline	*deen-*ya͜oo	電油
grease	wawng *ya͜OO*	黃油
an inner tube	*CHEH͜EH-ler N-TAH͜EE*	車輪胎
a jack	*CHEEN-GUN-*DI*NG*	千斤頂
a mechanic	*GAY͜EE-HAY GOO*NG*-yun*	機器工人
oil	*ya͜OO*	油
pliers	*kee M*	鉗
a pump	*BUM*	泵
a screwdriver	*law-SEE-PAH͜EE*	羅絲批
spark plugs	*FAW͜AW-FA-SUK*	火花塞
a tire	*soo-GAH͜OO CHEH͜EH-lerN*	樹膠車輪
tire patches	BO *TAH͜EE GAH͜OO-PEEN*	補汰膠片
tools	*GA-SAHNG*	傢生
a wrench	*woot-*doong *BANG-*ta͜oo	活動柄頭

Historic Soong Dynasty Figures - Tiger Balm Gardens

Aberdeen Fishing Houseboats Docked Towards Sunset

COMMUNICATIONS

TELEPHONE

English	Pronunciation	Chinese Writing
What central please?	nay‿ee DA‿AH HER BEEN-do AH	你打去邊度呀
Number please	nay‿ee YEE‿OO GAY‿EE DAW ho AH	你要幾多號呀
Repeat	joy GAWNG-GWAW	再講過
What number is calling?	nay‿ee ha‿ee GAY‿EE DAW ho AH	你係幾多號呀
Hang up your receiver	CHING nay‿ee GWA HAY‿EE deen-wa‿AH	請你掛起電話
The line is busy	yo‿oh yun GAWNG-GUN	有人講緊
Information	ngaw‿aw YEE‿OO mun-si-choo‿oo	我要問事處

English	Pronunciation	Chinese Writing
They do not answer	ker-day mo‿oh yun woo‿ee dahp	佢地冇人囘答
I will give you the chief operator	ngaw‿aw GEE‿OO GOONG-ta‿oo toong nay‿ee GAWNG	我叫工頭同你講
Here's your party	ker loy TANG deen-wa‿AH LAHT	佢來聽電話啦
Waiting?	nay‿ee DUNG-GUN LO‿OH MA	你等緊囉嗎
I will ring again	ngaw‿aw joy GEE‿OO ker LAHT	我再叫佢啦
I have a call for you	ya‿oo yun DA‿AH deen-wa‿AH BAY‿EE nay‿ee	有人打電話俾你
Can you hear me?	nay‿ee TANG-DO ngaw‿aw GAWNG MA	你聽到我講嗎
I cannot hear	ngaw‿aw TANG mm DO	我聽唔到

English	Pronunciation	Chinese Writing
Shall I continue to ring?	ngaw‿aw GA‿EE-jook GEE‿OO ker, HO‿OH mm HO‿OH AH	我繼續叫佢，好唔好呀
I will call you back	ngaw‿aw YUT juN joy GEE‿OO nay‿ee	我一陣再叫你
What number are you calling?	nay‿ee DA‿AH HER GAY‿EE DAW ho AH	你打去幾多號呀
Give me the number of ___	CHING nay‿ee GAWNG ___ GEH ho-SO BAY‿EE ngaw‿aw	請你講——嘅號數俾我
Long distance please	ngaw‿aw YEE‿OO cherng-to deen-wa‿AH	我要長途電話
What is the charge?	GAY‿EE DAW CHEEN AH	幾多錢呀
Reverse the charges	GEE‿OO GAW‿AW ta‿oo BAY‿EE CHEEN	叫個頭俾錢
Good-by	CHING AH	請呀

Numbers

NOTE: "Yee" is used in counting, but when you want to say two of anything (as "two men"), another word for "two" is used—"ler*ng*."

Numbers	Pronunciation	Chinese Writing
1	YUT	一
2	yee	二
3	SAHM	三
4	SAY	四
5	nn‿*ng*	五
6	look	六
7	CHUT	七
8	BAHT	八
9	GA‿OO	九
10	sup	十
11	sup-YUT	十一
12	sup-yee	十二
13	sup-SAHM	十三
14	sup-SAY	十四
15	sup-nn‿*ng*	十五
16	sup-look	十六
17	sup-CHUT	十七
18	sup-BAHT	十八

Numbers	Pronunciation	Chinese Writing
19	sup-GA͜OO	十九
20	yee-sup	二十
21	yee-sup-YUT	二十一
22	yee-sup-yee	二十二
30	SAHM-sup	三十
40	SAY-sup	四十
50	nn͜ng-sup	五十
60	look-sup	六十
70	CHUT-sup	七十
80	BAHT-sup	八十
90	GA͜OO-sup	九十
100	BAHK	百
1000	CHEEN	千
1,000,000	BAHK mahn	百萬

TELEGRAPH

I want to send a ——	ngaw͜aw YEE͜OO DA͜AH YUT GAW ——	我要打一個——
telegram	deen-BO	電報

English	Pronunciation	Chinese Writing
Give me a form	BAY‿EE JERNG seh-*eh* *deen*-BO-GEH JEE‿EE ngaw‿*aw*	俾張寫電報嘅紙我
Can I send a message to ___ (*name of place*)?	ngaw‿*aw* YEE‿OO DA‿*AH* *deen* HER ___ *DUK* mm *DUK* AH	我要打電去——，得唔得呀
You can	*DUK*	得
You can't	mm *DUK*	唔得
What is the charge?	GAY‿EE DAW CHEE*N* AH	幾多錢
Send it collect	HERNG SA‿OO *deen*-BO yun SA‿OO CHEE*N*	向收電報人收錢

MAIL

English	Pronunciation	Chinese Writing
Where is the post office?	ya‿oo-JING-GOOK ha‿EE BEEN-do AH	郵政局喺邊度呀
Where is the mail box?	SERN-*SERNG* ha‿EE BEEN-*do* AH	信箱喺邊度呀

English	Pronunciation	Chinese Writing
How much postage on this?	ya‿oo-FAH‿EE GAY‿EE DAW AH	郵費幾多呀
Registered	GWA‿AH ho	掛號
Registered with return receipt	GWA‿AH ho YEE‿OO woo‿ee-tee‿OO	掛號要回條
Insured	BO‿OH HEE*M*	保險
Insure for ___ (*money value*)	BO‿OH HEE*M* ___	保險——
Air mail	hawng-HOONG SERN	航空信
Second Class mail	yee-DUNG ya‿oo-geeN	二等郵件
Special Delivery	DUK-beet ta‿oo-da‿ee	特別投遞
What does it contain?	ler-ta‿oo ha‿ee MUT-yeh‿eh	裏頭係乜野
This package contains ___	ler-ta‿oo ha‿ee ___	裏頭係——
books	SOO‿OO	書
candy	tawNG	糖
clothing	YEE‿EE-fook	衣服
food	sik-mut	食物

English	Pronunciation	Chinese Writing
You may open it	nay_ee HAW_AW-yee_ee DA_AH HOY_EE ker	你可以打開佢
Perishable	woo_ee wah_ee-GEH	會壞嘅
Fragile (handle with care)	loy ya_oo BAW-LAY, SEE_OO-SUM	內有玻璃，小心
Give me ___ worth of stamps	CHI*NG* nay_ee BAY_EE ngaw_aw ___ see-DAHM	請你俾我一一士担
Send it	SOONG HER	送去
Mail this	GAY NEE-DEE	寄呢的

Chinese Tour Boat In Harbor, Skyline In Background

The Lippo Center

I.M. Pei's Bank Of China, Asia's Tallest Building

Food Shop In The Wanchai District Of Hong Kong

NUMBERS, SIZE, TIME, ETC.

AMOUNT

English	Pronunciation	Chinese Writing
A few *or* Several	GAY⌣EE GAW	幾個
Many	DAW⌣AW	多
Not many	mm DAW⌣AW	唔多
Very many	HO⌣OH DAW⌣AW	好多

ORDINAL NUMBERS

NOTE: For numbers 1—1,000,000, pages 69-70.

First	da⌣ee YUT	第一
Second	da⌣ee yee	第二
Third	da⌣ee SAHM	第三
Fourth	da⌣ee SAY	第四
Fifth	da⌣ee nn⌣ng	第五

English	Pronunciation	Chinese Writing
Sixth	da‿ee look	第六
Seventh	da‿ee CHUT	第七
Eighth	da‿ee BAHT	第八
Ninth	da‿ee GA‿OO	第九
Tenth	da‿ee sup	第十
Eleventh	da‿ee sup-YUT	第十一
Twelfth	da‿ee sup-yee	第十二

SIZE AND WEIGHT

English	Pronunciation	Chinese Writing
Small	SA‿EE	細
Large	dah‿ee	大
Medium	JOONG TING	中等
Long	cherng	長
Short	DOON	短
High	GO‿OH	高
Low	DA‿EE	低
Heavy	choong	重
Light	HANG	輕

TIME

English	*Pronunciation*	*Chinese Writing*
It's five o'clock	nn‿ng DEE*M*	五點
It's five ten	nn‿ng DEE*M* ler*ng* GAW *jee*	兩點兩個字
It's half past five	nn‿*ng* DEE*M* BOON	五點半
It's ten to six	nn‿*ng* DEE*M* su*p* GAW *jee*	五點十個字
Today	*G*UM-*yut*	今日
Yesterday	ku*m*-*yut*	琴日
Tomorrow	*T*ING-*yut*	聽日
In the ⎯		
morning	ser*ng*-nn‿*ng*	上午
afternoon	*ha*-nn‿*ng*	下午
evening	mah*n*-ta‿oo-*HUK*	晚頭黑
At ⎯		
dawn	*TEEN-MOON-GWAWNG*	天矇光
noon	AHN-ja‿oo	晏晝
midnight	BOON-yeh	半夜
night	yeh-mah*n*	夜晚

English	Pronunciation	Chinese Writing
Sunday	lah﹍ee – BAH﹍EE	禮拜
Monday	lah﹍ee – BAH﹍EE YUT	禮拜一
Tuesday	lah﹍ee – BAH﹍EE yee	禮拜二
Wednesday	lah﹍ee – BAH﹍EE SAHM	禮拜三
Thursday	lah﹍ee – BAH﹍EE SAY	禮拜四
Friday	lah﹍ee – BAH﹍EE nn﹍ng	禮拜五
Saturday	lah﹍ee – BAH﹍EE look	禮拜六
January	YUT yoot	正月
February	yee yoot	二月
March	SAHM yoot	三月
April	SAY yoot	四月
May	nn﹍ng yoot	五月
June	look yoot	六月
July	CHUT yoot	七月
August	BAHT yoot	八月
September	GA﹍OO yoot	九月

English	Pronunciation	Chinese Writing
October	su*p* y*oo*t	十月
November	su*p*-*YUT* y*oo*t	十一月
December	su*p*-yee y*oo*t	十二月
Week	lah‿ee – BAH‿EE	禮拜
Month	y*oo*t	月
One day	*YUT* yut	一日
Two days	ler*ng* yut	兩日
One week	*YUT* GAW lah‿ee-BAH‿EE	一個禮拜
Two weeks	ler*ng* GAW lah‿ee-BAH‿EE	兩個禮拜
One month	*YUT* GAW y*oo*t	一個月
Two months	ler*ng* GAW y*oo*t	兩個月

Historic Soong Dynasty Tableau - Tiger Balm Gardens

Hydrofoil In Hong Kong Harbor Heading To Lantau Island

Detail Of A Traditional Banquet Announcement Card

Water & Moon Guanyin, 11-12TH century

WEIGHTS AND MEASURES

Pronunciation	Chinese Writing	U. S. Equivalent (Approximate)
lerNG	兩	A little more than an ounce
GUN (=16 lerNG)	斤	About 1⅛ pounds
DAHM (=100 GUN)	擔	About 135 pounds
CHOON	寸	About 1½ inches
CHAK (=10 CHOON)	尺	A little more than a foot (about 14 inches)
jerng (=10 CHAK)	丈	About 12 feet
lay‿ee (=180 jerng)	里	⅓ of a mile

The following are sometimes used:

YING-lay‿ee	英里	English mile
GOONG-lay‿ee	公里	Kilometer (=⅝ of a mile)
ma‿oo	畝	Between ⅙ and ⅐ of an acre

Plaster Deity, Repulse Bay Beach

IMPORTANT SIGNS

Chinese Writing	English
停止	Stop
慢車	Go Slow
迂迴路徑	Detour
小心	Caution
危險	Danger
單行路	One Way Street
路不通行	No Thoroughfare
掘頭路	Dead End
靠右行	Keep to the Right
彎曲路	Dangerous Curve
火車路	Railroad
橋	Bridge
十字路	Crossroad
高壓電綫	High Tension Lines

Chinese Writing	English
男	Men
女	Women
廁所	Lavatory
禁止吸煙	No Smoking
禁止吐涎	No Spitting
汽車不得在此停留	No Parking
不准闖入	No Admittance
通行	Road Open
不通行	Road Closed
入口	Entrance
出口	Exit

A Hong Kong-Kowloon Star Ferry In The Harbor

ALPHABETICAL WORD LIST

English	Pronunciation
	A
accelerator	GA-*CHOOK*-HAY
address	*day*-JEE‿EE
afternoon	*ha*-nn‿*ng*
airfield	*FAY-GAY*‿EE-cherng
airplane	*FAY-GAY*‿EE
alcohol, rubbing	CHAHT *SUN*‿yoong-GEH FAW‿AW-JA‿OO
ambulance	GA‿OO-woo‿*oo-CHEH*
ankle	GERK-*JAH*NG
answer	*dahp*-AWN
antenna	*TEEN*-SEEN
apples	ping-GWAW‿*AW*
April	SAY *yoot*
arm	SA‿OO-BAY
August	BAHT *yoot*
auto	HAY-*CHEH*‿EH

English	Pronunciation
	B
back	BOO͜EE-JAK
baggage room	hahng-lay͜ee-fawNG
baked	HAWNG
bananas	HERNG-JEE͜OO
bandage	SA͜AH-BO
barber shop	TAH͜EE-ta͜oo-po͜oh
bathroom	SA͜EE-SUN-fawNG
beans	da͜OO
bed	chawng
beef	nga͜oo-yook
beer	BEH JA͜OO
beets	hoong law-bahk
belt	pay-dah͜EE
better	HOH͜OH-DEE-GEH
bicycle	DAHN-CHEH͜EH
black	HUK SIK
blanket	JEEN
blue	lahm SIK
boat	soon

English	Pronunciation
boiled	J*OO* *OO*
book	S*OO* *OO*
brake fluid	SAHT-*CHEH* EH-ya *OO*
brakes	JAH EE
brandy	but-*LAHN*-day EE JA *OO*
bread	meen-*BAH* *OO*
bridge	kee oo
bridle	ma ah-*GERNG*
broiled	SEE OO
brown	GA-*FEH* SIK
brush	ta oo-CHAH*T*
bulb, light	*DUNG*-dah*M*
bus	*GOO*NG-*goong* HAY-*CHEH* EH
bus station	*GOO*NG-*goong* HAY-*CHEH* EH-jah*m*
butter	nga oo-ya oo
buttons	na *OO*

C

cabbage	yeh-CHOY

English	Pronunciation
cable	TEET-lahm
camp	ying-fawng
candy	*tawNG*
canvas	fahn-BO
car	HAY-*CHEH*‿EH
carburetor	FA-ya‿oo-HAY
carefully	*SEE‿OO-SUM*
ceiling	wun-*GO*
certainly	*YUT*-ding
chains	TEET-*leeN*
chauffeur	*CHEH-FOO*
cheese	*CHEE-see‿EE*
cherries	*Y*ING-to
chest	*HOO*NG
chicken	*GA‿EE*
chocolate	*JOO-GWOO-LERT*
cigarette	*YEEN*-JA‿*EE*
city	sang
clams	hah‿*ee*
clerk	mun-*SOO‿OO*
cloth	BO
clothing	*YEE‿EE-fook*

Entrance And Facade To The Peninsula Hotel, Kowloon

The Famous Tea Room Lobby In The Peninsula Hotel

English	Pronunciation
clutch	lay-*hup*-HAY
coal	moo‿ee
coat	*SAHM*
coconuts	yeh-JEE‿*EE*
coffee	GA-*FEH*
color	ngahn-*SIK*
comb	*SAW*
controls	GW*OON*-JAH‿EE
cook	faw‿*aw-ta*‿*OO*
cotton	*yerk*-meen-*FA*
cream	*gay*-LEEM
cup	*BOO*‿*EE*

D

danger	nga‿ee-HEE*M*
dates	JO‿*OH*
dawn	*TEEN-MOON-GWAWNG*
day	*yut*
December	*sup-yee* *yoot*
deck	*gahp-bahN*
deep	*SUM*
dentist	nga-FAW *YEE-SUNG*

96

English	Pronunciation
Diesel oil	ya‿oo-*JA*‿AH *ya*‿*OO*
direction	FAW*NG*-HERNG
disinfectant	*SEE*‿OO-*dook* *yerk*-SER
doctor	*YEE-SUNG*
donkey	lo-JA‿*EE*
driver	*YUT* GAW HAY-*CHEH-FOO*
drug store	*yerk*-fawng
dry	*GA*WN
dry cleaned	*GA*WN-SA‿*EE*

E

English	Pronunciation
ear	yee‿*ee*-JA‿*EE*
east	*DOO*NG
eggs	*GA*‿*EE-dahN*
elbow	SA‿*OO-JAH*NG
electric wire	*deen*-SEEN
electrician	*deen*-HAY *GOO*NG-yun
engine	*GAY*‿EE-HAY
engineer	*GOONG-ching*-SEE

English	Pronunciation
Engineers	*GOONG-BING*
envelopes	SERN-*FOONG*
equipment	HAY-*hah⌣ee*
evening	mah*n*-ta⌣oo-*HUK*
eye	ngah*n*

F

face	*meen*
family	*OOK*-kay⌣*ee*
far	y*oon*
fare	*lo*-FAH⌣EE
father	lo⌣*oh*-da⌣*oo*
February	*yee yoot*
few, a	GAY⌣*EE* GAW
firearm	*CHERNG*
fire extinguisher	*meet*-FAW⌣*AW*-HAY
fireman	FAW⌣*AW*-FOO
firewood	chah⌣*ee*
first-aid packet	GA⌣OO-*GUP* yerk-doy⌣*EE*
fish	*yoo⌣OO*
flag	kay

English	Pronunciation
flashlight	*deen*-SA‿OO-D*UNG*
flat	ping
food	*sik-mut*
foot	GERK
fork	CHA
Friday	lah‿*ee*-BAH‿EE nn‿*ng*
fried	CHAH‿*OO*
friends	pung-ya‿*oo*
fuel tank	ya‿oo-SE*R*NG

G

garage	*CHEH*‿EH-*fawNG*
gas	*dook* HAY
gasoline	*deen*-ya‿oo
glass	*BAW-LAY BOO‿EE*
gloves	SA‿*OO*-TO
good	HO‿*OH*
grapes	*po*-tah‿ee-JEE‿*EE*
gravel	*sak*-JA‿*EE*
gray	*FOO‿EE SIK*

English	Pronunciation
grease	wawng *ya̠OO*
green	*look SIK*
grocery	*jahp-faw-po̠OH*
guide	*YUT* GAW yun DAH̠EE *lo*
guideposts	*lo*-pah̠ee

H

hammer	*cheR*
hand	*SA̠OO*
handkerchief	*SA̠OO*-GUN-JA̠*EE*
hat	*mo̠OH*
head	ta̠oo
heavy	*choong*
help	GA̠OO *mang* AH
here	*NEE-do*
high	*GO̠*OH
hills	*SAH*N-JEE̠*EE*
hip	SEE̠*OO*-YEEM-*GWUT*
horn	HAY-*CHEH̠*EH la-*BA*

English	Pronunciation
horse	ma‿*ah*
horseshoe	ma‿*ah*-tah‿ee-TEET
hotel	le*r*-GWOO*N*
husband	lo‿*oh-*GOO*NG*

I

ice	S<u>OO</u>T
ink	*muk*-SE*R*
inner tube	*CHEH*‿EH-*ler N-TAH*‿*EE*
insecticide	SAHT-choong-*yerk*
interpreter	*ch<u>oo</u>n-wa*‿*AH*
iodine	*DEEN JA*‿*OO*
iron	
corrugated iron	S*I*NG-TEET
sheet iron	TEET-*bahN*

J

jack	*CHEEN-GU*N-DI*NG*
January	*YUT y<u>oo</u>t*
jaw	*ha*-pa
July	*CHUT y<u>oo</u>t*

The Bank of China

New Apartment Towers Across From Aberdeen Harbor

English	Pronunciation
June	look y<u>oo</u>t

K

key	SAW‿*AW*-see
kilometer	*GO*ONG-lay‿*ee*
knee	*SUT*-ta‿oo
knife	*DO*

L

ladder	*TAH*‿EE
lakes	*woo*
lamb	yerng-*yook*
languages	*wa-AH*
large	*dah‿ee*
larger	*dah‿ee-DEE*-GEH
laxative	SEH-*yerk*
left	JAW‿*AW*
leg	TE*R*
lemons	ning-*MOONG*
lentils	BEE*N*-da‿*oo*
lettuce	*SAH*NG-CHOY

English	Pronunciation
light	*DUNG*-FAW‿*AW*
lobsters	*loong*-HA
long	*cherng*
low	*DA*‿EE
lumber	*mook-lee*‿OO

M

Madam	AH-SU*M*
mail	SERN
mangoes	*MA*WNG-GWAW‿*AW*
many	*DAW*‿AW
map	*day*-to
March	*SA*HM *yoot*
matches	FAW‿*AW*-*chah*‿*EE*
May	nn‿*ng* *yoot*
meat	*yook*
mechanic	*GAY*‿EE-HAY *GOO*NG-yun
medium	*JOO*NG TI*NG*

English	Pronunciation
message	SERN-*geeN* *or* ching-BO
messenger	ch*oo*n-DA‿AH-y*oo*n
midnight	BOON-yeh
milk	nga‿oo-*NAH‿EE*
Miss	SEE‿*OO*-JEH‿*EH*
Monday	lah‿*ee*-BAH‿EE *YUT*
money	CHEE*N*
month	GAW *yoot*
more	*DAW-DEE*
morning	ser*ng*-nn‿*ng*
mother	lo‿*oh*-mo‿*OH*
motor	*MAW-da‿AH*
motorcycles	*deen-DAHN-CHEH*
mountains	*SA*H*N*
mouth	HA‿*OO*
movie	YI*NG*-HAY-*yoo N*
Mr.	*SEEN-SAHNG*
Mrs.	AH-SU*M*
muddy	na‿ee-BAHN *DAW‿*AW

English	Pronunciation
mud puddles	na‿ee-TU*M*
mule	ler

N

nails	*DA*NG
near	ku*n*
neck	GA*NG*
needle	*JUM*
night	yeh-mah*n*
noon	AHN-ja‿oo
north	*BUK*
northeast	*DOONG-BUK*
northwest	*SA‿EE-BUK*
nose	bay-*GAW*
November	sup-*YUT* y*oo*t
number	ho-SO
nurse	*HA*WN-woo‿*oo*

English	Pronunciation
	O
observer	*GWOO*N-CHAHT-y<u>oo</u>n
obstructions	*yeh⌣eh* JAW⌣*AW-ngoy*
octane rating	*S*UN-y<u>oo</u>n *ding-lert*
October	*sup y<u>oo</u>t*
oil	*ya⌣OO*
oil rating	ya⌣oo *ding-lert*
oil viscosity	ya⌣oo-GEH *LEE*M-SING
orange (*color*)	*chahNG* wawng *SIK*
oranges	*chahNG*
overcoat	*dah⌣ee-LAH⌣OO*
oysters	*SA*HNG-ho
	P
pants	*foo*
paper	JEE⌣*EE*
passable	hahng-*D UK*
passes	*SA*HN-*lo*
paths	SEE⌣OO-*lo*
peaches	*to⌣UH*
pears	*lay⌣EE*
pencil	y<u>oo</u>n-*BUT*

English	Pronunciation
pepper	woo-*JEE*‿OO-FU*N*
perishable	woo‿*ee* wah‿ee-GEH
pick	chaw-*ta*‿*OO*
pigeon	*TOO*NG-SERN-GAH*P*
pillow	JU*M*-ta‿oo
pilot	*FAY*‿EE-hahng-y<u>oo</u>n
pineapples	*BAW*‿AW-law
pins	*da*‿*ee*-ta‿oo-J*UM*
place	*day*-*FA*WNG
plane	*FAY*-*GAY*‿EE
plate	*deeP*
please	CHI*NG* nay‿*ee*
pliers	*kee*M
plums	*moo*‿*EE*
police station	GI*NG*-CHAHT-GOO*K*
pork	J<u>OO</u>‿<u>OO</u>-*yook*
porter	*YUT* GAW yun D*A*H*M* yeh‿*eh*
post office	ya‿oo-JING-GOO*K*
potatoes	*soo*-JA‿*EE*
potholes (*roads*)	TU*M*

A Night View Of Hong Kong's Famous Skyline And Harbor

Fishermen At Cheung Chau Island, A Fishing Village

English	Pronunciation
powder, talcum	SAW*NG*-*SUN*-FU*N*
pressed	TAWNG
private	*B*ING
propeller	*CHEH*⌣EH-*yeeP*
pump	*BUM*
purple	*CH*ING-*leeN SIK*

Q

quick *or* quickly	*FAH*⌣EE-*DEE*
quilt	pay⌣*ee*
quinine	*GUM-GA*⌣*EE-nahp*

R

radio	mo⌣*oh*-SEEN-*deen*
radio equipment	mo⌣*oh*-SEEN-*deen yoong*-BU*N*
radio repairman	mo⌣*oh*-SEEN-*deen SA*⌣OO lay⌣*ee*-y*oo*n
radio set	mo⌣*oh*-SEEN-*deen*-*GAY*
radio station	mo⌣*oh*-SEEN-*deen*-toy
railroad	FAW⌣*AW*-*CHEH*⌣EH-*lo*
raincoat	y*oo*⌣*oo*-*YEE*

112

English	Pronunciation
raw	SAHNG
razor	SO‿OH-*pah*‿OO
razor blades	TA‿EE-*SO-DO*-PEEN
receipt	SA‿OO-tee‿oo
red	hoong SIK
reflector	fahn-seh-*GAY*
repaired	SA‿OO-JING
restaurant	*fahn*-GWOON
rice	*fahn*
right	ya-*oo*
river	haw
road	*lo*
roasted	SEE‿OO
rocky	sak-ta‿oo *DAW*‿AW
room	*fawNG*
rope	sing-SAWK
runway, surface of the	PAH‿OO-*do* day-meen
ruts	*CHEH*‿EH-*lerN*-YUN

Dancers In Royal Costume

Deity In Three Buddha Temple In Central Hong Kong

English	Pronunciation
	S
saddle	ma‿ah-AWN
salt	yeem
sand	SA‿AH
Saturday	lah‿ee-BAH‿EE *look*
scarf	GA*NG*-G*UN*
scissors	GAH‿OO-JEE*N*
screwdriver	*law*-SEE-PAH‿EE
September	GA‿OO *yoot*
several	GAY‿EE GAW
sheets	pay‿ee-DAHN
shirt	SERT-SAHM
shoelaces	hah‿ee-*dah*‿EE
shoes	hah‿ee
short	DOON
shoulder	BAWK-ta‿oo
shovel	*chahN*
sick	bang
Sir	SEEN-SAH*NG*

English	Pronunciation
slow *or* slowly	*mahn-DEE*
small	SA‿EE
soap	*FA*H*N-GAHN*
socks	*mut*
soup	*TA*WNG
south	nahm
southeast	*DOO*NG-nahm
southwest	*SA*‿EE-nahm
spark plugs	FAW‿*AW-FA-SUK*
specialty	*JIK-wah‿ee*
speed limit	*KWA*‿EE-DING-GEH *CHOOK-do*
spinach	*BAW*‿AW-CHOY
splints	*gahp-bahN*
spoon	chee-*GUNG*
springs	SE*R*-ch<u>oo</u>n
squash	JEET-*GWA*
stable	ma‿*ah*-fawng
stamps	*see-DAHM*
station	
bus station	*GOO*NG-*goong* HAY-*CHEH*‿EH-jah*m*
railroad station	FAW‿*AW-CHEH*‿EH-jah*m*

English	Pronunciation
steak	nga‿oo-*PA*
stomach	to‿*oh*
strawberries	yerng-moo‿ee
sugar	tawng
Sunday	lah‿*ee*-BAH‿EE
sunglasses	*JEH*‿EH *yut-ta*‿*OO*-GEH ngah*n*-GA*NG*
supplies	*GWUN*-*SER BUN*
sweater	*LAHNG-SAHM*
switchboard	*deen*-JAH‿EE-*bahN*
switchboard operator	*deen-wa SEE-GAY*

T

tail	may‿ee
tailor shop	*SA*‿*EE-JAWNG-po*‿*OH*
tan	*S*U*M*-wawng *SIK*
taxi	*DIK-see*‿*EE*
tea	cha
telegram	*deen*-BO
telephone	*deen-wa*‿*AH*

English	Pronunciation
telephone exchange	deen-wa‿AH-GOOK
telephone lines	deen-wa‿AH SEEN
tent	JERNG-mawk
there	GAW‿AW-do
thread	SEEN
throat	ha‿oo-loong
Thursday	lah‿ee-BAH‿EE SAY
ticket	FAY
timetable	see-GAHN-BEE‿OO
tire	soo-GAH‿OO CHEH‿EH-lerN
tire patches	BO TAH‿EE GAH‿OO-PEEN
today	GUM-yut
toilet	CHEE-SAW‿AW
toilet paper	CHO‿OH-JEE‿EE
tomatoes	FAHN-keh‿EH
tomorrow	TING-yut
tools	GA-SAHNG
tooth	nga
toothbrush	nga-CHAHT

English	Pronunciation
toothpaste	nga-*GO*
tooth powder	nga-FU*N*
tourniquet	JEE‿*EE*-H<u>OO</u>T-*dah*‿*EE*
towel	mo-*GUN*
town	sang
train	FAW‿*AW*-*CHEH*‿EH
truck	JOY-*joong* HAY-*CHEH*‿EH
Tuesday	lah‿*ee*-BAH‿EE *yee*
turnips	law-*bahk*

U

undershirt	DA‿*EE*-SAHM
undershort	DA‿*EE*-*foo*
United States	may‿*ee*-GWAWK
U. S. Consulate	may‿*ee*-GWAWK *ling*-see-GWOO*N*
U. S. Government	may‿*ee*-GWAWK JING-FOO‿*OO*

V

| vegetables | CHOY |

English	Pronunciation
vinegar	CHO
visibility	see-gah‿ee

W

wagon	SAY-lern-*CHEH*
washed	*SA‿EE*
water	SE*R*
watermelon	*SA‿EE-GWA*
Wednesday	lah‿*ee*-BAH‿EE *SA*H M
week	lah‿*ee*-BAH‿EE
well (*for water*)	JA*NG*
well done	*sook-DEE*
west	*SA‿*EE
wet	*SUP*
white	*bahk SIK*
wife	lo‿*oh*-paw
wind	
wind direction	*day-meen FO*ONG-HERNG
wind velocity	*day-meen FO*ONG-CHOOK
wine	JA‿*OO*
wings	*yik*
wire	TEET-SEE*N*

English	Pronunciation
woods	*soo*-lum
wrench	*woot*-doong *B*A NG-ta‿oo

Y

year	neen
yellow	wawng *SIK*
yesterday	kum-*yut*

Large Chinese Junk In Full Sail In Hong Kong Harbor